306.89 BIS
Bishop, Keeley, 1963
Family break-up /
ASV

Just the Facts

Family
Break Up

Keeley Bishop
Penny Tripp

Heinemann Library
Chicago, Illinois

Customer Service 888-454-2279
Visit our website at www.heinemannlibrary.com

Designed by Jamie Asher
Originated by Ambassador Litho Ltd.
Printed and bound in China by South China Printing Company

07 06 05 04 03
10 9 8 7 6 5 4 3 2 1

Library of Congress Cataloging-in-Publication Data
Bishop, Keeley, 1963-
  Family break up / Keeley Bishop and Penny Tripp.
      p. cm. -- (Just the facts)
Summary: Discusses what makes a family in today's world, how that
definition has changed over time, reasons why families break apart, how
to deal with the changes, and religious, ethical and legal views of
divorce and family break up.
Includes bibliographical references (p.) and index.
  ISBN 1-4034-0819-X (Library Binding : hardcover)
 1. Divorce--Juvenile literature. 2. Broken homes--Juvenile
literature. [1. Divorce. 2. Family. 3. Remarriage.] I. Tripp, Penny,
1949- II. Title. III. Series.
  HQ814 .B48 2003
  306.89--dc21
                                        2002010940

Acknowledgments
The author and publisher are grateful to the following for permission to reproduce copyright material:
Cover photograph: Kim Naylor/Collections (top); Ute Klaphake/Photofusion (bottom); ImageState (left).
p. 5 Ariel Skelley/Corbis; p. 6 Mary Evans Picture Library; p. 7 top Kim Naylor/Collections; pp. 7 bottom, 8, 9, 31 John Birdsall
Photography; pp. 10–11 Erich Lessing/AKG London; p. 13 Popperfoto; pp. 14–15 Bill Ray, Timepix/Rex Features; pp. 17, 28, 29,
37 Ute Klaphake/Photofusion; p. 19 SIE Productions/Corbis; p. 20, 43 Sally and Richard Greenhill; pp. 21, 27 Christa
Stadtler/Photofusion; pp. 23, 50–51 Paula Solloway/Format; pp. 25, 35 Jenny Matthews/Network Photographers; p. 33 Graeme
Peacock/Collection; p. 34 Michael Ann Mullen/Format; p. 36 Skjold Photographs; p. 38 Nigel Hawkins/Collections; p. 39 Ulrike
Press/Format; p. 41 Paul Baldesare/Photofusion; p. 42 Liz Stares/Collections; p. 45 Rex Features; pp. 46–47 Will and Deni
McIntyre/Science Photo Library; p. 48 Julian Hirshowitz/Corbis.

Our special thanks to Pamela G. Richards, M.Ed., for her help in the preparation of the book.

Some words appear in bold, **like this.** You can find out what they mean by looking in the glossary.

Contents

Family Break Up

Families in the 21st century come in all shapes and sizes. Gone are the days when "family" automatically meant married parents and their children.

One hundred years ago, family break up was much less common than it is now. When people got married, they expected to stay married to the same person until one of them died. They had children who often lived with them until the children found husbands and wives of their own.

People still get married, have children, and live together happily ever after, but the fact is that many of them do not. Nearly half of all U.S. marriages end in **divorce,** and so do many marriages in the United Kingdom. Today's children are much more likely than their grandparents to experience the break up of their family. Roughly one in four of them will spend at least part of their childhood with only one parent.

The family you live with right now might be your mother and father, you, and some brothers and sisters. Another typical modern family could be a mother and father and just a single child. One friend might live with her mother and her mother's new **partner** and their children. Another might live with his father and brothers and sisters. You may also know people living with a grandparent or an aunt or an older cousin who looks after them.

Confusing?

Things can get even more confusing. Even families that seem happy and settled can fall apart. A family member may die or leave. Parents may separate because they can no longer live together. Whatever the reasons behind family break up, its impact on everyone involved can be enormous.

For some people, it is only slightly less painful than dealing with death. They experience the same kind of feelings when their family breaks up as they do when someone close to them dies— disbelief, anger, and sadness. For others, it may be easier.

What Is a Family?

There have been families as long as there have been people. They are different all over the world, but until as recently as one hundred years ago, most children in **Westernized societies**—in the United States, the United Kingdom, and Australia for example—lived with their father and mother. They might have had many brothers and sisters. In 1800, the average number of children in a U.S. family was seven; by 1900, it was between three and four; and by 2000, it was two. This kind of **nuclear family** is much less common now.

Children today might live with one, two, or more adults. A pair of adults in a family group might be married to each other, or they might not. They might be one male and one female, or both of the same sex. One of the adults might be the child's **biological parent** or both of them might be. Some children live in families parented by adults who are not biologically related to them, because the children are **adopted** or in **foster** care. Others live with members of their **extended family**—their grandparents or an aunt or older cousin. In some countries, such as in Russia, China, and southern Asia, most family units are still large.

Large, close-knit families bound together by marriage—like this American family one hundred years ago—are less common today.

An alternative lifestyle

All over the world, many families join together to live and work in **communes.** Different communes exist for different reasons. Some people live in them because they think they offer a better way of sharing responsibilities, including caring for children, than more traditional family units. Others do so because they want to live and work with people who have the same goals in life. Many communes are based on shared religious ideas, while some focus more on what it means to live together and support other people as members of a group.

Children brought up in such groups may think of themselves as having many parents, rather than just two biological parents. They have close, family-type relationships with many people who are not related to them.

"A family is somewhere you live and are loved and cared for."

(Rupinder, age 14)

Today's parents are less likely to be married for life than their grandparents were.

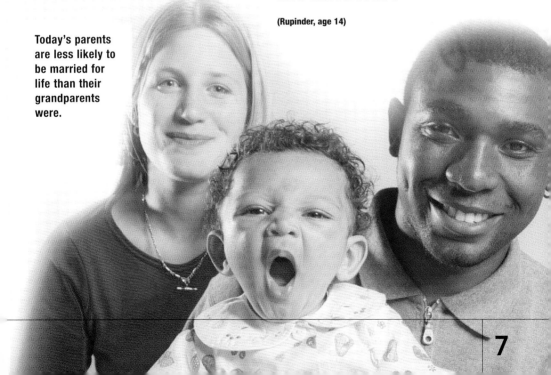

7

What Is a Family Break Up?

Some family break ups happen after a long period of unhappiness. Others are sudden. All are difficult to handle, and everyone experiences them in different ways.

Separation and divorce

Parents who decide to separate may do so for one reason or for many. They may no longer share the same interests or feel the same way about each other as they once did. Disagreements may have turned into constant arguments. One might find the other's behavior difficult to deal with, or have met someone else they want to live with.

When an adult leaves after a long period of unhappiness and anger, those remaining may feel relieved that they have gone. If the break up is sudden, they are more likely to be angry, confused, and bewildered.

Children often feel that their parents' break up is somehow their fault. They may understand very little about what has happened, and the remaining adult may be so upset or angry that he or she cannot easily talk about it with them.

Death or disappearance of a family member

Some families are broken up by death. Some deaths happen suddenly, while others are expected. Someone dying after a long illness may leave the rest of the family feeling sad, but relieved that he or she is no longer in pain. The sudden death of a family member can lead to feelings of grief, anger, or sadness that can be very difficult to express.

Sometimes, people simply leave. There may have been an argument, or the person who left may have felt that he or she just could not continue living as part of the family any longer. The person may have felt unloved, or felt that he or she

Some families stay together forever, but others may not.

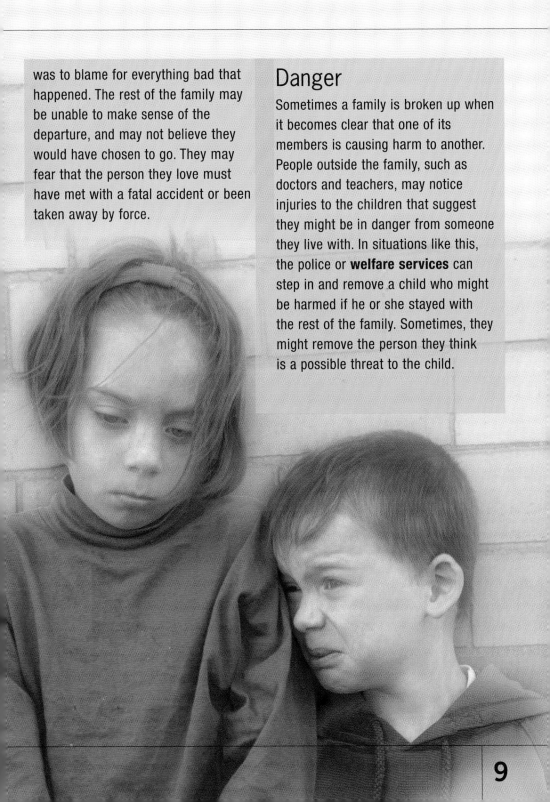

was to blame for everything bad that happened. The rest of the family may be unable to make sense of the departure, and may not believe they would have chosen to go. They may fear that the person they love must have met with a fatal accident or been taken away by force.

Danger

Sometimes a family is broken up when it becomes clear that one of its members is causing harm to another. People outside the family, such as doctors and teachers, may notice injuries to the children that suggest they might be in danger from someone they live with. In situations like this, the police or **welfare services** can step in and remove a child who might be harmed if he or she stayed with the rest of the family. Sometimes, they might remove the person they think is a possible threat to the child.

The First Families

Why did family groups first appear?

There have been people on Earth for almost two million years. Our species has survived where others have not, despite the fact that in some ways it seems poorly equipped for survival. Many animals fend for themselves almost from the moment of birth, but our young need care for many years if they are to make it into healthy adulthood. They rely heavily on their parents' **nurturing** instinct—a strong desire to look after offspring—and survival skills. Without these they die, and so does the species.

Early humans lived wherever they could find food, water, and shelter. Their world was full of powerful predators. Even a relatively strong adult could be killed by a mammoth or a saber-toothed tiger. Our ancestors had no food unless they caught it, killed it, picked it off a plant, or dug it up.

Males, females, and their young probably banded together with other small family groups because that way they were more powerful, and therefore more likely to survive. A single **nuclear family** would have had no chance if one of its adults became sick, was injured, or died.

Families through time

Slowly, over tens of thousands of years, living conditions changed. But family groups still formed the basis for societies all over the world. Deep-rooted instinctive, emotional, and social ties kept them together.

In some cultures, it was the parents of a nuclear family who had primary responsibility for

Ancient Egyptian paintings and sculptures often show husbands and wives with their arms around each other.

the welfare of their own children. Others organized themselves into societies based on **communes,** where children were cared for by the group as a whole rather than by the child's **biological parents.** If a parent left the group for any reason, children still had others they could depend on until they could take care of themselves.

By 5,000 years ago, the ancient Egyptians had written laws about what a family was, and had penalties for those who broke them. People who ignored or did not conform to the rules laid down by their religion, or who just acted differently from those around them, had a price to pay.

Families in ancient Egypt
• A girl was usually married by the time she was fourteen. Her husband was probably around age twenty.
• There was no official marriage ceremony. People were considered married when they started living together, and **divorced** when they split up.
• Some couples' marriages were arranged by their parents, especially if both families were rich and powerful and wanted to form an alliance with each other. Others married because they loved each other.
• Important men often had many wives, and some kings had hundreds.
• The chief wife was her husband's equal. She ran the house, owned all the household goods, and had her own servants.

Family Break Up in History

One hundred years ago, a typical family in the United States, the United Kingdom, or Australia was usually made up of a married couple and their children. Men were generally the ones responsible for making decisions in public life, such as in business and politics. They usually only got married when they had enough money to support a wife and children. They might inherit this money when their parents died or, more often, have to work for it. Women rarely worked outside the home. Their job was to run the household using the money their husband supplied and raise the children.

Marriage was considered to be the foundation for a solid family life, and anybody who had a sexual relationship outside marriage was looked down on. Women who became pregnant without a husband were often sent away from home until their babies were born, and were thought to have brought shame on their families. Their **illegitimate** children had no father's name on their birth certificate and few legal rights.

Marriage may have been the only way anybody could have a proper sexual relationship and **legitimate** children one hundred years ago, but that did not mean all marriages were happy. An unhappy marriage could be legally ended through **divorce.** This process was difficult and involved having to prove that one partner—usually the wife—had been guilty of unacceptable behavior.

A woman's **adultery**—having a sexual relationship outside her marriage—was sufficient reason for a husband to divorce her, but she could not divorce him for the same reason! A divorced woman's children became her ex-husband's property, and he could stop her from ever seeing them. Adulterers and **divorcees,** especially women, were thought to be a bad influence on children and incapable of caring for them properly. Getting married for a second time, unless a previous husband or wife had died, was almost unheard of.

During the 20th century, large numbers of men left home, sometimes for years on end, to fight for their countries during World War I and World War II. Families broke up while they were away, sometimes forever. Many women filled the jobs the men left open and, instead of depending on

their husbands for financial support, earned their own money for the first time. Those whose husbands were killed brought up their children as best they could.

Even in the 1950s, society and its laws still decreed that marriage was forever, and that there was no place for sex or children outside it. Child-care experts said that parents who separated or divorced would damage their children, and people believed them.

During World War II, women who had never worked outside their homes took on jobs previously done only by men.

Family Break Up Since 1960

Families in the middle of the 20th century began to have fewer children than before. From 1800 to 1960, the number of children in an average U.S. family decreased from seven to just more than three. This decrease in family size was due to many factors. Many couples no longer relied on their children to work on farms or in factories to help support the family. Also, many more women were working outside the home, and some were even earning enough to be financially independent. They no longer had to rely on finding a suitable husband to look after them, because they could look after themselves.

Marriage and children, though, still went hand-in-hand. Many young people were pressured into marriage because their relationship had led to an unplanned pregnancy.

The 1960s

Boys and girls in their late teens in the 1960s had more options than to stay at home and wait to get married in order to become independent of their parents. They could find jobs and earn a living, or go to college and continue their education. It became more common for young people to move away from home before they were married. They no longer had to rely on their parents for money.

By the late 1960s, people could have sexual relationships without having children, because the **contraceptive** pill was widely available, even to unmarried women. It was gradually becoming more acceptable for men and women to live together without being married, and getting married was becoming more of a choice than a necessity. Women also wanted the same freedom to get **divorced** if a marriage did not work out.

The 1970s onwards

Since the 1970s, fewer people have chosen to marry. There are twice as many single-parent families today as there were in previous years. Some are that way because parents have divorced, others because people have chosen to bring up their children without being married. By 2000, roughly one in four U.S. children lived with a single parent—84 percent of them with their mothers.

Young people in the 1960s not only started to dress differently from their parents, but to think differently, too. Many of the old rules were changing.

Family change in the United States

	1970	2000
Family groups with children	30 million	37 million
Single-mother families	3 million (12% of all families)	10 million (26% of all families)
Single-father families	393,000 (1% of all families)	2 million (5% of all families)

(Source: U.S. Census Bureau, 2001)

Current Trends

So many families have experienced a break up of some kind that it is no longer considered unusual. Statistics show that all the industrialized nations are experiencing similar trends. Family units are breaking up and becoming smaller, and fewer children are being born.

Marriage is becoming less popular, and almost half end in **divorce.** There are more than one million divorces each year in the United States—about 3,000 divorces per day.

Families today

Single-parent families are twice as common today as they were in the 1970s. Today, an estimated twenty million U.S. children—roughly one-quarter of all the children in the nation—live in a single-parent family. At one time, the children of divorcing parents were automatically thought to be better off living with their mothers, with their fathers giving financial support and having **contact** or visiting rights. More fathers are now successfully arguing that they are just as capable of raising children on their own as mothers are. Divorced mothers and fathers are increasingly encouraged to share responsibility for the children they brought into the world.

Being divorced does not make it impossible to marry again, or to live with someone else. Families formed when this happens—**stepfamilies**—are becoming more common. **Blended families** are formed when a parent goes on to have children with a new **partner,** who may also have children from a previous relationship.

Some children are born to parents who cannot take care of them. Young mothers and fathers who are still in school, for example, may want a better life for their child than they feel they can give. Other parents may suffer from a physical or mental illness that makes it difficult for them to care for a child. In these kinds of situations, a child can be **adopted** or placed in a **foster** family. The law is changing in some countries to allow adoption by unmarried couples who can show that they can offer a child a stable home and meet his or her needs.

"I live with my mom during the week, and with my grandparents on weekends. I see my dad on Sundays."

(Michael, age 14)

Today, many children live with their mother for part of the week and their father for the rest of the week.

Reasons Why Families Break Up

Family break up can happen after a long period of unhappiness, or very suddenly. A family may split apart after years of arguments and violent disagreements, in spite of many attempts to keep it together. Either separately or together, parents may look for outside help—such as from **counselors** or members of their church—before making a final decision to split up. Another family might experience the sudden, and permanent, departure of one of its members. A parent or child could die, for instance, or might suddenly leave because of feeling that he or she can no longer stay.

Drifting apart

Shared interests, ideas, and values are the basis for many relationships. But interests and ideas can change, or differences of opinion become more important than they once were. A couple might gradually realize that they no longer have anything in common, and that there does not seem to be any point in staying together.

Wanting to be with someone else

Even people who think they are happy together can fall in love with someone else. They cannot imagine living without this new person, even though they know that leaving their present **partner** will be difficult and painful. Falling in love is not something that people choose to do, but it is a powerful feeling and hard to ignore.

Wanting to go in different directions

When two people get together, they tend to agree on the direction their lives will take. They know what kind of work they want to do, how they will spend their free time, and what their long-term ambitions are. Their plans cannot take into account something they haven't even thought of—such as the realization that they cannot get what they really want if they stay with their partner.

Failure to agree

Many couples argue about money, but it is not the only thing they disagree about. When they find little common ground on anything, and arguments arise all the time without being settled, life becomes so difficult that splitting up may be the only option. Other families may accept that their arguments are a normal part of family life and remain strong and settled in spite of them.

Abuse

Most people agree that it is never acceptable to use physical violence against a child, or for one adult to use violence against another. Violence within a family is often hidden, and can sometimes go on for a long time without anyone outside knowing about it. Sexual **abuse** of one family member by another can also be hidden. People who abuse alcohol or other drugs can become aggressive and violent towards other family members or neglect their parental responsibilities. Breaking up a family is sometimes the only way to keep family members safe and well.

Some parents argue all the time and still have a strong relationship, but others become frustrated and angry if they feel they cannot agree on anything.

The "Normal" Family

"Normal" families in 21st-century industrialized societies reflect the fact that a family break up is far more common than it was 50 years ago. Families arrange themselves in so many different ways after a break up that it is hard to know what normal is. In the United States, 32 million children—44 percent, are living in a so-called "nontraditional family."

When couples separate, they sometimes feel a lot of bitterness and anger towards their ex-**partner** and find it hard to agree on who their children should live with. In some situations it is obvious where the children will be better off. In other situations, it is not so clear. Today, though, children's opinions are listened to more often than they used to be.

Parents who no longer live with their children are usually encouraged to see them regularly. Parents do not stop being a parent when they **divorce,** unless they are thought to be a danger to the child.

Living with mom

Roughly 84 percent of children live with their mother after their parents split up, sometimes in the same family home as before, sometimes in a new one. More than four million children in the United States, for example, live with their mother in their grandparents' house. Many see their fathers regularly. Others do not.

Living with dad

It is becoming more common for children to live with their father after a separation. For many years it was thought that fathers could not care for their children properly. This belief is changing as men become more involved in parenting and more women take on demanding full-time jobs.

Stepfamilies

When parents divorce to form a relationship with someone new, their new partner may have children of his or her own. If they then marry, the two families join together and the children find themselves living with stepbrothers and stepsisters.

Joint custody

Some children live with their mother for some of the time and with their father for the rest. Their parents share responsibility for the child's care just as they did before they broke up.

Flexible arrangements

When parents divorce, they have to decide where their children will live and who will look after them. These arrangements do not have to stay the same forever, and can be changed later as long as everyone involved agrees.

Leonie

Leonie's mom started a relationship with a man who was also divorced. The man had two children of his own who lived with their mother, but who stayed with him every other weekend. In the beginning, this was on the same weekends that Leonie was away seeing her dad.

"I used to get really mad at first," says Leonie. "Ian and Lucy came and stayed in my room, and got to do fun things with their dad and my mom. My room was always a mess, and I know they went through my things. I hated it. I couldn't believe my mom would let them do this."

Leonie's mom and dad switched weekends, and relationships improved. Leonie now joins in the family's activities and no longer feels that she is missing out.

Changes

Family is the most important and powerful thing in the lives of most children. If one of their parents dies, or their mother and father split up, or someone they care about leaves their family, children may think that the love and stability they knew have gone forever. Although it can feel like that at first, most children eventually get used to the kind of changes a family break up brings. If family life has meant a lot of arguments and unhappiness, a break up can be a relief, and things may seem a lot better afterwards.

Frequently asked questions

Faced with many changes, children and young people ask questions. Some are very difficult to answer, and parents have to deal with them while they cope with their own fears about what the future holds.

Who will be responsible for me?

If one parent leaves, children sometimes fear that they are going to end up completely on their own. They may even be afraid that the other parent will disappear, too.

Where will I live? Do I have any choice?

If the parent who leaves is the one they feel closest to, children may be deeply troubled at the thought of not going with them. They may fear having to choose between two people they love. When they associate a parent with violence or **abuse,** they may be afraid that they will be forced to stay with that parent or have to see him or her even if they do not want to.

What will I say to my friends?

Children often think that their own family is the only one that has ever been through a break up. They may not realize that they know many other people who have been through the same thing.

Children may worry that their friends will see them and their family as weird or embarrassing. If the break up means a move out of the area, they may be afraid that they will never see their friends again.

Young people whose lives are changing can find it helpful to talk to friends. Girls often find this easier than boys.

Is it my fault?

Although parents say their children are never to blame for a family break up, children do not always see it that way. They remember times when they made a parent angry or when they seemed to be the reason for a disagreement. They think that if only they had been good, this would not be happening. But families do not break up because children have misbehaved.

What will happen to my pets?

Worrying that one change will automatically lead to others, children may feel that they are going to lose everything that is important to them.

Will we be poor?

Children may worry about whether they can still have treats, trips, and birthday presents, especially if the parent they will be living with does not work outside the home.

Can I see or talk to my Mom or Dad when I want?

Children who are close to a parent who is leaving want to know if they can stay in touch. Telephone calls, e-mails, letters, and visits can all help, and children need to know whether they can make the first move rather than just wait. On the other hand, a child who has had bad experiences with the parent who is leaving needs reassurance that they will not be forced to see that parent if they do not want to.

Will we live as a family again?

A child who loves both parents and cannot really understand why they are breaking up may hope for a long time that the family will get back together again.

E-mail can be a good way of sharing news with family members who live somewhere else.

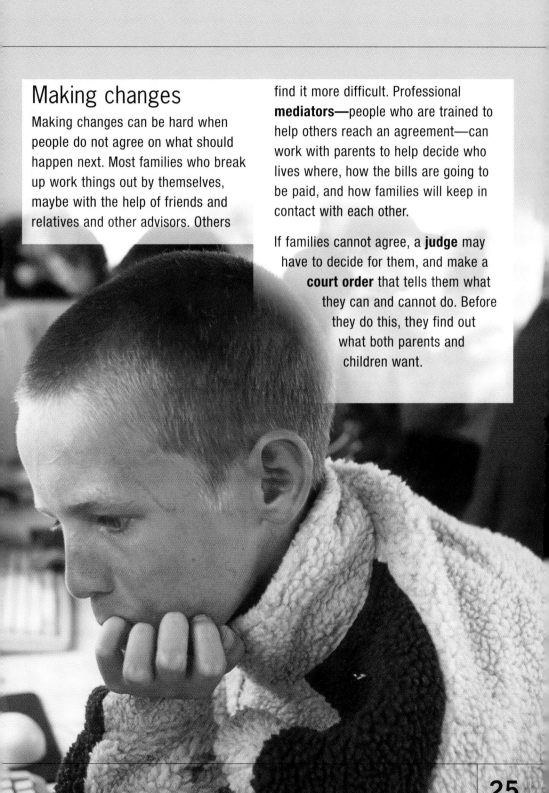

Making changes

Making changes can be hard when people do not agree on what should happen next. Most families who break up work things out by themselves, maybe with the help of friends and relatives and other advisors. Others find it more difficult. Professional **mediators**—people who are trained to help others reach an agreement—can work with parents to help decide who lives where, how the bills are going to be paid, and how families will keep in contact with each other.

If families cannot agree, a **judge** may have to decide for them, and make a **court order** that tells them what they can and cannot do. Before they do this, they find out what both parents and children want.

Common Reactions

Most young people who have experienced a separation from one or both parents clearly remember the moment they realized what was happening. How they react depends on the reasons for the separation, how old they are, and the atmosphere surrounding the break up—fear, sadness, relief, or hostility. Although a family break up may feel frightening and difficult at first, most people find that things get easier over time.

Birth to two years old

Children under two years old are highly dependent on their parents. They are especially close to the person who they spend the most time with. These children do not understand what is happening to their family, but they are acutely aware of the stress and anxiety of those around them. If a person who usually cares for them is gone for any length of time, they miss and worry about that person.

Two to five years old

Separation can be a major shock to children in this age group. Anger, sadness, and anxiety are common reactions, and children as young as this can show signs of **depression.**

They may show their distress by behaving as they did when they were younger, doing things they seemed to have outgrown, such as bedwetting and thumb-sucking. Some start using "baby talk" again. Preschool children make sense of their world in very different ways from older children, and may make up stories to explain things they do not understand.

Six to eight years old

The children in this age group seem to have the hardest time coping with a family break up. They commonly experience great sadness and feelings of being unlovable. They often feel that the departing parent is rejecting them. They may find it hard to concentrate at school, and start behaving in ways that alert friends, teachers, and parents to the fact that they are feeling bad. They cannot explain how they feel in words. They want their family back the way it was, and often do and say things to try and make this happen.

Nine to twelve years old

At this age, most children have friends and interests outside their family. Although their family is still very important to them, it is no longer their only world. They feel shock and sadness when their family breaks up, and these feelings often turn to anger against the parent who leaves. Although they understand more about what is happening than younger children do, they can still feel powerless, helpless, and rejected. They worry about the future and what will happen to them. Their schoolwork often suffers. Unlike younger children, however, they can put their feelings into words and accept help and reassurance from those around them.

Teens

Young people over the age of twelve are usually more independent from their families, and more influenced than younger children by reactions from their friends. They tend to distance themselves from both parents while they try to understand their feelings. They worry about what the break up will mean for their future. Will they be able to stay at the same school? Go to college? Keep their current friends? If they have been aware for a long time that relationships within the family were difficult, they may feel relief that the stress is over.

Feeling lonely and sad is a very common reaction to a family break up.

Long-term reactions

Ten years after a family break up, young people report many mixed feelings about what happened. How they manage to cope with it seems in all cases to be directly related to the way their parents behave. An atmosphere of parental cooperation rather than conflict means that children can adjust to the changes in their own way and their own time. Constant parental fighting leaves children with long-term feelings of sadness and insecurity, and they find it hard to feel good about themselves.

❝My mom and dad got divorced when I was ten. I didn't know why. But when I look back on it now, I can see they were miserable together and things weren't going to get any better. It seemed terrible at first, but then things settled down. My dad's remarried and my mom's got a boyfriend. They both seem happier than they did when they were together.❞

(Lora, age 21)

29

Social and Welfare Services

Family break ups sometimes involve more people than just those who are directly involved. Neighbors, teachers, or health workers who deal regularly with family members may become worried about their health, their safety, or how they are behaving. In some cases they may report their concerns to the police or others who are legally responsible for the welfare of people in the community. These people may then step in.

Some of these people work for government-funded social and **welfare services.** Others are employed by locally-based public authorities to make sure that individuals and families, especially children, get help when they need it.

Why do welfare services get involved?

Parents who are physically or mentally ill may not be able to care for their children properly. Others may have drug or alcohol habits that affect how they behave. Some may have violent tempers that they cannot control. When they are angry, they may lash out at people close to them and hurt them. Some adults are **pedophiles.**

They are sexually attracted to children rather than people their own age, and try to involve children in illegal sexual relationships.

In situations like these, where children are neglected or hurt, welfare services can call on the power of the law to remove children from the family to protect them and keep them safe.

How do welfare services get involved?

Those who come into contact with children, such as teachers and health workers, are trained to recognize the signs of neglect or **abuse.** If they suspect that a child is not being cared for properly, they may report their concerns to welfare services or the police and explain why they are worried. Sometimes neighbors or friends alert the authorities.

Outsiders sometimes step in to help sort out family difficulties. This kind of help is not always easy to accept.

There are special police units whose job it is to help families in trouble. They protect children and other people at risk, often working closely with welfare services. They may suggest classes or **counseling** sessions for parents who find it hard to care for their children, but who want to stay together as a family. They have the power to remove a family member who is in danger or who is a threat to others. In situations where children are thought to be in immediate or serious danger, they can be removed from their family. This can only happen after a proper investigation, and may involve presenting a **judge** with evidence in **court.**

Removing children from their families is a last resort. It is done when they are thought to be in real danger from neglect or harm if they remain. If their own family environment is not safe, children then need to be placed in a new home. There may be family friends or relatives who can offer them one. If not, they may be placed in a **foster** home or they may be **adopted.**

Foster care

Foster families are people willing to care for children who are not their own. These families take care of children until they can go back to their own homes or be placed in a permanent one elsewhere. People who want to be foster parents are carefully checked by **welfare services** to make sure that they can offer children a safe and secure place to live. In return, the families get financial support from the welfare service that places children with them.

Some foster parents have children of their own, but others do not. Children are often placed with foster parents who live close by, so that they can see members of their family and their friends and keep going to the same school. Some foster children may stay only until they can go back to their own families, or until they move in with a family that wants to adopt them.

Adoption

Children who cannot live with their own family may be adopted, and become a permanent and legal part of a new family. They may be adopted by someone in their **extended family.** Children becoming part of a **stepfamily** are sometimes adopted by their stepfather or stepmother. Other children may be adopted by individuals or couples completely unrelated to them. These people have said they want to bring the children up as their own, and have shown that they can offer the right kind of home.

After a Family Break Up

Once a family has broken up, it is unlikely to come back together again in the same shape. The difficulties and differences that cause parents to break up do not disappear just because the parents have separated or have a piece of paper that tells them they are **divorced.** The children of separated parents may at least see their **absent parent** sometimes, but it can take a long time for a family to get used to living without a parent who has died.

In the first year after a break up, everyone must make practical and emotional adjustments to a new way of life. It can be a confusing and unsettling time, but it does not last forever.

Living with one parent and visiting the other

Children used to living with two parents can find it hard to adjust to seeing one of them all the time, and the other only occasionally. Sometimes formal arrangements, such as in a divorce agreement, set rules about who can see each other. There may be rules about how often this can happen, where visiting takes place, and how long each visit can last. Children can feel torn between their parents, especially if there has been disagreement over who they are going to live with.

It takes time to get used to a new school and to spending more time with one parent than another.

34

Everybody reacts to family break up in their own way.

Having two homes

Children may have two homes. They may live in one most of the time, and visit the home of the other parent. Some find this exciting and different, others find it confusing. Many children find it difficult to leave one of their homes to go to the other.

Changing schools

Older children may find a move and a change of school especially difficult, as their lives outside the family are important to them. School means stability and friendships, and moving to a new one may leave them feeling unsettled and lost.

Not seeing one parent

Children may be prevented from seeing a parent because **welfare services** thinks they might be at risk if they do. Their feelings in this situation may be complex. Children may still love a parent, even if the parent has been neglectful or has harmed someone in the family. On the other hand, everybody may be glad the parent is no longer involved with the family, but still find it hard to adjust to their absence.

New Families

Stepfamilies

Single parents may remarry or form new long-term relationships that bring children into **stepfamilies.** The new **partner** becomes a stepparent to the children, and their children become stepbrothers and stepsisters.

Life in a stepfamily can be very difficult at first. Children tend to compare their new stepparent to their "real" parent. They may have to share a home with people they do not know well. They also have to share their parent with the parent's new partner, and with other children. There may be new family rules to get used to. As the initial strangeness wears off and relationships form, things usually get better.

Foster homes

Children and young people removed from their families by outside agencies, such as **welfare services,** often do not understand why they have to leave. They may find themselves separated from their brothers and sisters as well as their parents, and living with a **foster** family they do not know. It might be just for a few weeks or for a longer period of time. The children are often angry and confused. They think that people are not listening to them and are not interested in what they want. Their parents may be angry and resentful that the family has been broken up, but unable or unwilling to make the changes that would mean it could come together again.

Adoptive homes

Children may be **adopted** by their stepparents, or by people previously unknown to them who can offer the kind of stable, settled home their own parents cannot provide. Fitting into any new family can be hard at first, especially if a child has already experienced a lot of changes in his or her family life. Social workers may sometimes visit to help sort out any difficulties.

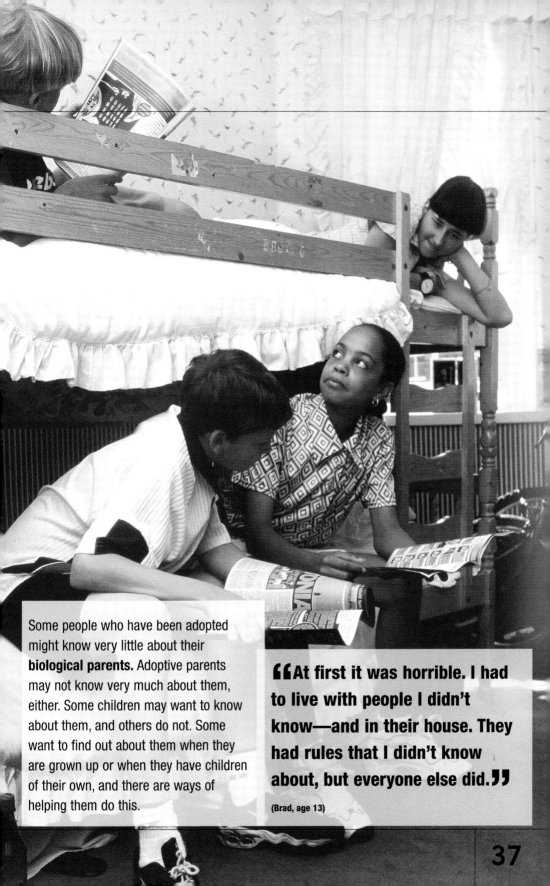

Some people who have been adopted might know very little about their **biological parents.** Adoptive parents may not know very much about them, either. Some children may want to know about them, and others do not. Some want to find out about them when they are grown up or when they have children of their own, and there are ways of helping them do this.

"At first it was horrible. I had to live with people I didn't know—and in their house. They had rules that I didn't know about, but everyone else did."

(Brad, age 13)

Keeping in Touch

A family break up can mean that one household becomes two, and children see less of the parent they no longer live with. The official name given to the times when children see their **absent parent** is **contact** or **visitation.**

Many young people say that regular contact with both parents helped them deal with the emotional upheaval surrounding the family break up. Continued contact helps them to understand that a parent still loves them even if they live somewhere else.

Ways of keeping in touch

Separated families keep in touch in many different ways. Children might visit an absent parent once a week or every weekend or once a month. Some people keep in touch through phone calls, e-mails, and letters. Some families regularly exchange videos and photographs, while others use websites and webcams.

Why does contact help?

Children who do not have regular contact with one of their parents can grow up with an unrealistic view of what that parent is really like. They might come to imagine the parent as all good or all bad. Few parents truly fit into these two categories, and a child in regular contact with both parents will be able to see the true picture.

Continued contact with an absent parent helps children feel part of a loving family, even if all the members of it do not live together. Staying in touch means that

family members can continue
to share experiences and keep each
other up-to-date with what is
happening to them. It is especially
important if brothers or sisters—or
maybe even grandparents or other
family members—are now
living with the absent parent.

Saying goodbye at the end of
a visit can be difficult, but
usually gets easier over time.

When contact is difficult

When parents separate or **divorce,** they may find it hard to agree on when, where, and how children and the **absent parent** see each other. Difficulties in arranging contact times usually have more to do with the parents' relationship with each other than anything the children do. Even when an agreement has been reached, some parents find it hard to stick to it. One parent may feel so angry with the other that he or she cannot encourage and support the child's relationship with the other parent. Another parent may be so upset by what has happened that he or she cannot bear to let the children go anywhere near the former **partner.** Some children find themselves passing messages between their parents because the adults find it so hard to talk directly. This changes over time, but is common in the beginning.

Kids in the middle

In this kind of situation, children may hear one parent say many critical things about (or to) the other. "Of course, she's always late!" and "You'd rather go out with your friends than see the children anyway" might be some of the comments that children hear. Other comments may be directly addressed to the children, such as "Your father was never any good at keeping his promises." To children, this kind of talk can often sound as if one parent is trying to turn them against the other. Sometimes this is true, but more often it is an expression of how hurt and angry the parent feels.

Children sometimes feel as if one parent is trying to get them to spy on the other. This can make the child unwilling to say anything about the other parent for fear of causing an argument or upsetting anybody. Children can end up feeling like ping-pong balls bouncing between separated parents. There may be nothing they can do to keep them both happy at this stage, but many children try.

No contact

There may be times when it is impossible for children to see one of their parents. The child may be at risk of violence or other harm, for example. Or one parent might find it too difficult. As the child gets older, though, contact may become possible again.

"Before visitation was decided, I spent my weekends on the train traveling between my parents because I didn't want to upset anyone."

(Jack, age 15)

Religious Views

It is becoming more common for people to have children without being married, but most of the world's major religions think that marriage is the best way of making sure that children are born into stable and long-lasting families. Within every religious community, however, there are some who believe that parental separation and **divorce** are always wrong, and others who think that it depends on individual circumstances.

In most countries, a legal marriage can be ended by divorce if certain conditions are met. These vary from place to place. Religious marriages can usually be ended, too, but those who belong to some religious communities can find themselves rejected—even by their families—if they divorce.

Christians

Customs vary from country to country, and between the different Christian religions. In the United States, for example, some strict religions expel **divorcees** who marry for a second time. A Roman-Catholic marriage can only be dissolved under certain rare conditions. The Greek Orthodox Church disapproves of divorce, but does not forbid it. In the United Kingdom, legally divorced members of the Church of England were unable to remarry in a church for many years, while those who belonged to the Church of Scotland could. Now ministers look at individual cases before making a decision.

Although more and more couples are choosing not to marry, most religions still believe that marriage is the best way of ensuring that children are cared for properly. But will a marriage last? Nearly half of them now end in divorce.

Muslims

Customs and ideas vary between one branch of Islam and another, and from country to country. There are strict rules about how property should be divided, and how children should be cared for. Divorcees are not prevented from marrying again, but women who do so are frowned upon in some cultures.

Jews

Within each branch of Judaism, as in all religions, there are strict and more lenient groups. All recognize divorce, and there is no ban on remarriage.

Hindus

Marriage is an unbreakable holy bond for Hindus, rather than a legal contract as it is for many other religions. Most communities recognize legal divorce, but some find it hard to believe that a divorced woman, or even a woman whose husband has died, could even think of marrying again.

Sikhs

Like Hindus, Sikhs see marriage as a holy bond but recognize divorces granted in accordance with the law of the land.

Ethical Questions

Ethics are the moral values upon which nearly all civilizations, societies, and communities are based. They attempt to provide people with answers to questions such as "What is right?"; "What is wrong?"; "What is good?"; and "What is bad?" It is often very difficult to come up with the right answer to this kind of question.

Are two parents always better than one?

Some children are born to mothers and fathers who are committed to raising their offspring together. Some live happily with both parents, others with one. Some parents successfully bring up their children outside a traditional family structure, either by themselves or with a **partner** of the opposite or same sex.

A two-parent family may not automatically be a good thing. If one parent physically **abuses** the children, for example, or spends money on drugs or gambling rather than food, the family may be better off without that person.

Should families always stay together?

At one time, a family stayed together no matter what happened or how miserable its members were. Women and children were the property of their husbands and fathers, and men could treat them as they saw fit. If wives and children were abused or neglected, there was often nowhere else for them to go. Two hundred years ago, a woman who was married by age 18 might have given birth to 10 children by the time she was 30. But life expectancy was much shorter then, and as many as one in five children died in infancy.

Things are very different today, and some people argue that rules and customs should not remain the same when people's lives have changed so dramatically. Medical advances, reliable **contraception,** better nutrition, and better housing have all meant that people are living longer and having fewer children than they used to. Women are no longer expected to spend their entire lives raising children and taking care of the home. Some earn far more money than the men they choose to have children with, and some are choosing to have no children at all.

Is there such a thing as a proper family?

Trends in **Westernized societies** show that families are now much more likely to break up than they were even twenty years ago. Families also take on many different forms. Today's babies may grow up happily within a number of different family groups, or with a single parent. One hundred years ago, family change might only have happened when a parent died.

Even royal families experience family break ups. The future king of England, Prince Charles, and his current partner, Camilla Parker-Bowles, are both **divorced.** Public opinion in the United Kingdom is divided as to whether they should marry and about whether she should become the queen if they do.

Help During a Family Break Up

A family at risk of breaking up, or one that has broken up already, is going through a very difficult time. Family members may be feeling guilty, **depressed,** or frightened. Sometimes they may be feeling a mixture of all these emotions and more. They may have little money. Some may be homeless, others physically hurt or mentally ill. Some feel that what happens to their family is nobody's business but their own, and are unwilling or unable to ask for help. Others, especially children, often do not know where to get help.

Friends and relatives

Young people whose family is breaking up can feel very alone. They may be able to talk to an aunt, uncle, or grandparent about what's happening at home, but sometimes worry that they are being disloyal. They might also be afraid that what they say will lead to trouble for them or for another family member. Often they find that talking to someone they know and trust helps them feel less lonely and more able to cope.

When people do not agree, an outsider can sometimes help.

Outside help and advice

Children may find it easier to talk to someone completely outside of their family. A trusted teacher or youth **counselor** may be able to offer advice or put children in touch with someone who can help. Schools and community centers have information about a wide range of support services available to children and families. In the United States, schools offer assistance through special support groups, counselors, or student-assistance programs.

There are many organizations that give emotional and practical support to children and adults dealing with family problems.

Counseling and support

Health centers and doctors' offices can also put people in touch with people who will listen to their problems and help them figure out what to do next. These counselors work directly with individual children or parents, with couples, and with families, depending on what type of help is needed.

Support groups, sometimes organized and run by local parents or members of religious communities, can also be helpful. Their meetings may be listed in local newspapers or advertised on local radio stations.

Legal help

Some people will never reach agreement without help because their situation is complicated, or because they are hostile to each other. Many people today have the chance to use the services of a **mediator**—someone who is not on anybody's side, who knows the law, and who can help the couple work together rather than fight things out.

If a couple cannot agree about what should happen to their children, their house, or their money, they can each instruct **lawyers** to negotiate for them and speak for them in **court. A judge** listens to both sides of the argument and reaches a legal decision.

Family members often turn to grandparents for help during a family break up. Children often find grandparents easier to talk to than parents.

Family Break Up and the Law

Throughout the world, special laws protect the rights of family members. Details vary from one country to another. In the United States, the family laws vary from state to state. Family law covers situations in which the police or **welfare services** can step in to protect children and young people thought to be in danger. It can be used to prevent an **abusive** person from making contact with other family members. It also covers **divorce.**

Divorce

Divorce is the legal ending of a marriage. In order to get a divorce, a couple has to meet certain conditions and follow a set legal procedure. Conditions and procedures vary. Divorcing couples with children have to show that the children's needs for a

Children's thoughts and feelings are taken into account by the courts when families break up.

home, financial support, education, and **contact** with the parent they will not be living with have all been taken into account. The views of the children are also heard. Some couples agree on all of the arrangements concerning their children's future, and these are included as part of their divorce.

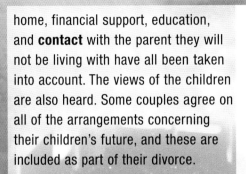

What if parents cannot agree?

Judges have the power to make decisions for any parents who cannot agree about the legal matters regarding their children. These decisions are **court orders.** They may determine who the children will live with. They may determine arrangements for visiting, telephoning, and having contact with an **absent parent** or other family members. Judges can also make decisions about how much money one parent should give the other.

If one parent is violent or abusive, a judge can make him or her leave the family home and not come back, or forbid the parent from being abusive again. Adults who do not do what the judge orders can be punished.

Information and Advice

Many organizations and groups offer free advice and confidential counseling services for anyone dealing with family problems. In addition, school counselors have information about resources for young people.

Family break up contacts

Center for Children's Justice, Inc.
5082 East Hampden Avenue, Suite 223
Denver, CO 80222
(303) 282-1634
http://www.childrensjustice.com
This nonprofit organization is dedicated to protecting the rights of children and preserving the rights of children's access to both parents.

Children Now
1212 Broadway, 5th Floor
Oakland, CA 94612
(510) 763-2444
http://www.childrennow.org
This organization works as an independent voice for children. They work to translate the nation's commitment to children and families into action.

Children's Rights Council
2201 I ("Eye") Street, Suite 200
Washington, D.C. 20002
(202) 547-6227
http://www.vix.com/crc/index.html
The CRC assists children of separation and divorce through advocacy and parenting education.

Joint Custody Association
10606 Wilkins Avenue
Los Angeles, CA 90024
(310) 475-5352
http://www.jointcustody.org
This organization deals with issues such as child support reform and child custody practices.

National Association of Child Advocates
1522 K Street, NW, Suite 600
Washington, D.C. 20005
(202) 289-0777
http://www.childadvocacy.org
There are 63 member organizations in 47 states that this national organization can put people in touch with. Their mission is to provide a voice for children and their families at both the national and local levels.

Parents Without Partners
401 North Michigan Avenue
Chicago, IL 60611
(800) 637-7974
http://www.parentswithoutpartners.org
PWP is an international organization that provides help for people facing parenthood after being divorced, separated, or widowed.

More Books to Read

Aydt, Rachel. *Why Me?: A Teen Guide to Divorce and Your Feelings.* New York: Rosen Publishing Group, Inc., 1999.

Calhoun, Florence. *No Easy Answers: A Teen Guide to Why Divorce Happens.* New York: Rosen Publishing Group, Inc., 2000.

Goldentyer, Debra. *Child Abuse.* Chicago: Raintree Publishers, 1998.

Goldentyer, Debra. *Divorce.* Chicago: Raintree Publishers, 1998.

Isler, Claudia. *Caught in the Middle: A Teen Guide to Custody.* New York: Rosen Publishing Group, Inc., 2000.

Johnson, Linda Carlson. *Everything You Need to Know about Your Parent's Divorce.* New York: Rosen Publishing Group, Inc., 1998.

Kuehn, Eileen. *Divorce: Finding a Place.* Mankato, Minn.: Capstone Press, Inc., 2001.

Leibowitz, Julie. *Finding Your Place: A Teen Guide to Life in a Blended Family.* New York: Rosen Publishing Group, Inc., 2000.

Glossary

absent parent mother or father who does not live with their child

abuse ill-treatment of someone by hurting them (physical abuse), forcing them to have sexual contact against their will (sexual abuse), not caring for them properly (neglect), or harming them emotionally (emotional abuse)

adoption legal process leading to a child being adopted and raised by a person—or persons—who is not his or her biological parent

adultery sexual relationship between a man with a woman other than his wife, or between a woman with a man other than her husband

biological parent mother or father of a child—that is, the mother who conceived and gave birth to the child or the man whose sperm helped create the child

blended family family formed when a parent goes on to have children with a new partner, who may also have children from a previous relationship

commune alternative to traditional family life in which unrelated people and their families live and work together as a close-knit group based on shared ideas or goals

contact child's right or opportunity to stay in touch with an absent parent, or an absent parent's right or opportunity to communicate with his or her child

contraception artificial or natural means of preventing pregnancy

counselor person trained to give advice and help to others

court legal body with the power to hear cases and make decisions on matters of law

court order official decision made by a court, with penalties for anyone who does not abide by it

depression long-lasting mental state that brings with it feelings of deep sadness and worthlessness

divorce legal ending of a marriage

divorcee person who is legally divorced

extended family family members less closely related to someone than his or her mother, father, brothers, and sisters. An extended family may include cousins, uncles, aunts, and grandparents.

foster to temporarily house and care for a child by a family that is not his or her own

illegitimate child born to parents who were not married to each other at the time of the child's birth

judge legally qualified public official with the power to preside over legal cases and make decisions

lawyer trained professional who can advise people on legal matters and speak for them in court

legitimate child born to parents legally married to each other

mediator person who helps those involved in disputes to reach an agreement

nuclear family someone's closest relatives, such as parents, brothers, and sisters

nurture to encourage the development of a child

partner either member of a couple in a relationship

pedophile criminal adult who befriends young children because he or she wants illegal sexual relationships with them

stepfamily family formed when one or two adults with children form a lasting relationship

visitation child's right or opportunity to stay in touch with an absent parent, or an absent parent's right or opportunity to communicate with his or her child

welfare service people employed by the local, state, or federal government to provide help that ensures the well-being of individuals and families in need

Westernized society society that shares the kind of customs, laws, and values common in the Western—as distinct from the Asian or African—world

Index